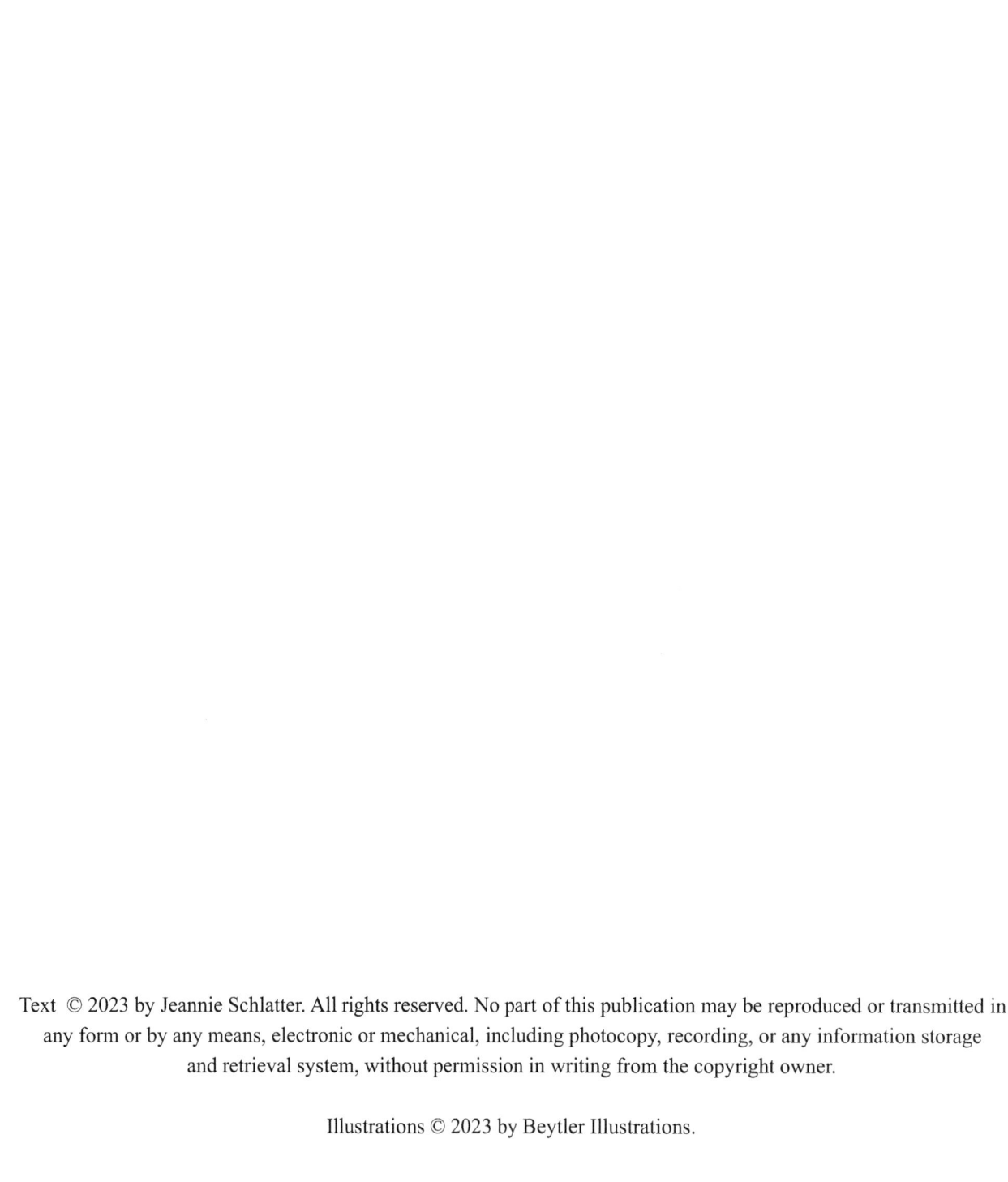

Text © 2023 by Jeannie Schlatter. All rights reserved. No part of this publication may be reproduced or transmitted in any form or by any means, electronic or mechanical, including photocopy, recording, or any information storage and retrieval system, without permission in writing from the copyright owner.

Illustrations © 2023 by Beytler Illustrations.

A Picture Book

Written by Jeannie Schlatter

Illustrated by SASH

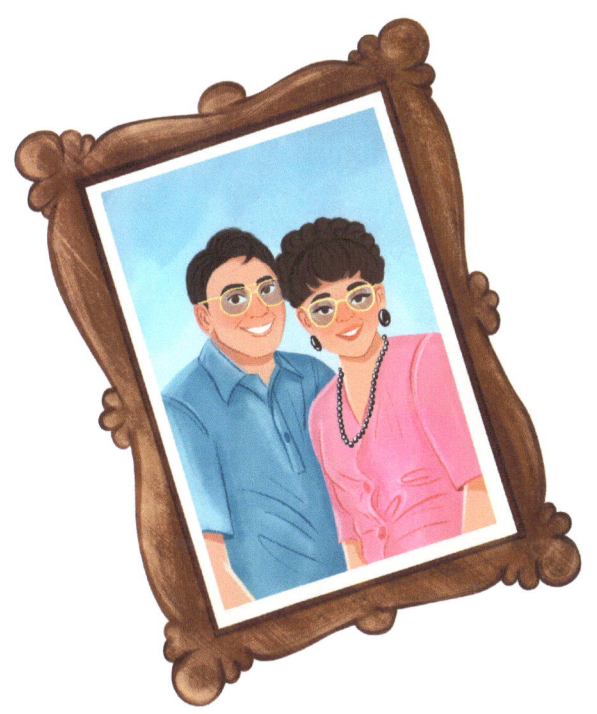

This book is dedicated to my Mom & Dad, for instilling in me the love of photography & capturing sweet memories. And to my family, for enduring & encouraging my picture taking & blessing me with all the captured and uncaptured memories that I will always treasure!

Thank you for allowing me to take so many pictures and Thank you for all the pictures you have sent!!! I love you!

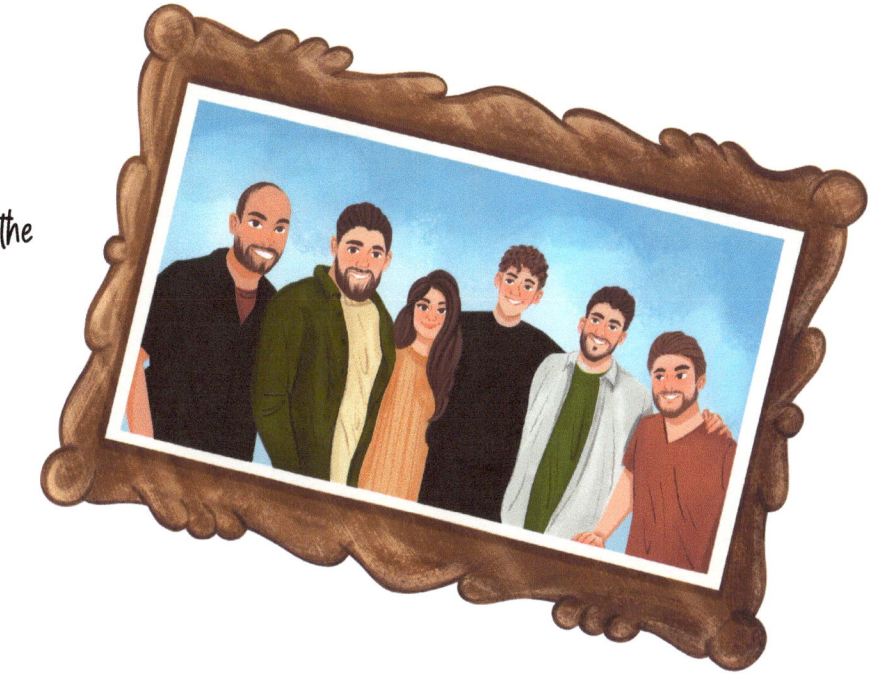

When Jean Ann was young, her Mom LOVED to take pictures!!
"Say Cheese!!" She would say. She always took pictures of people
& things she loved.

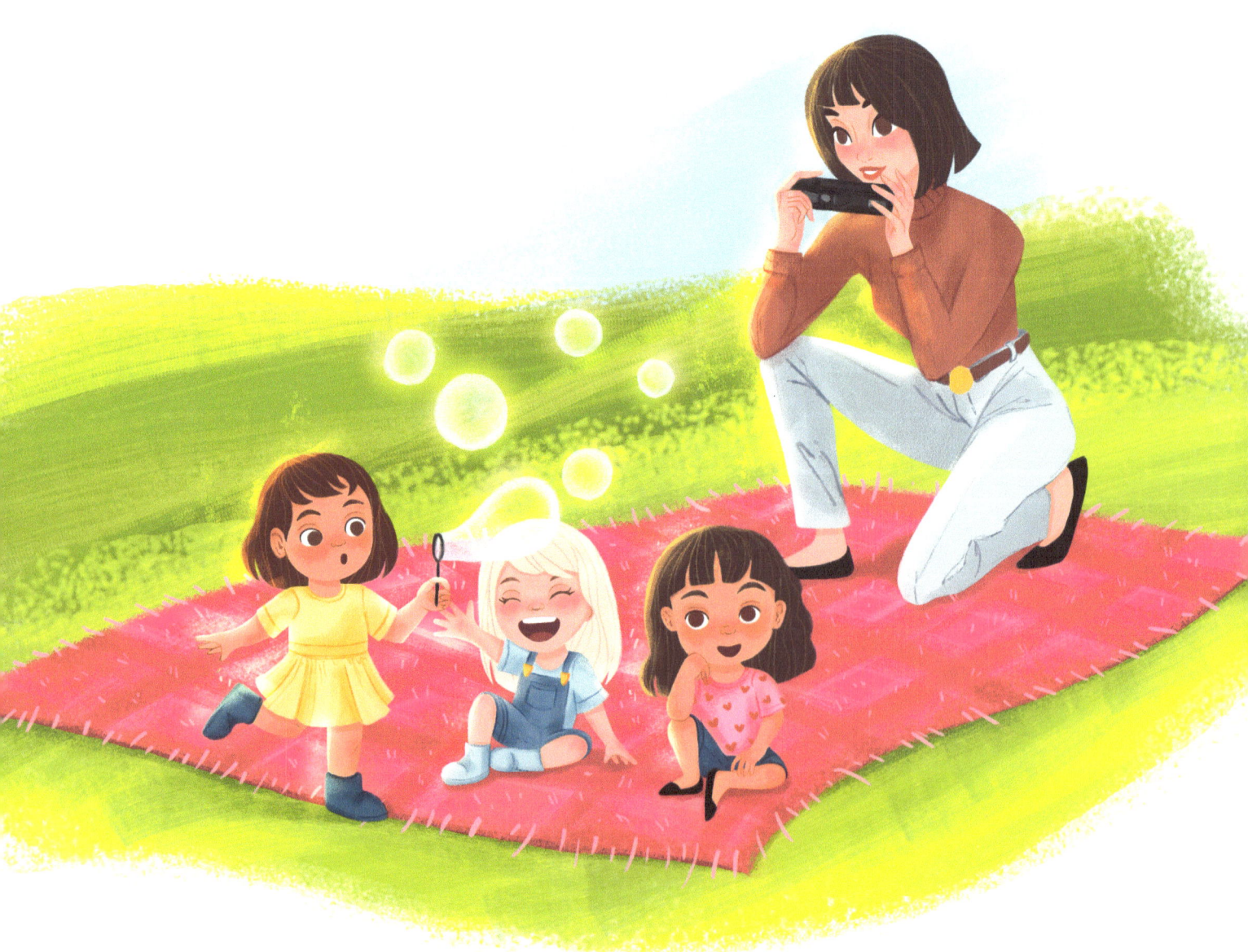

Sometimes, Jean Ann and her Mom would just sit and look through Photo Abums together. They would talk about who was in the picture and when & where it was taken.

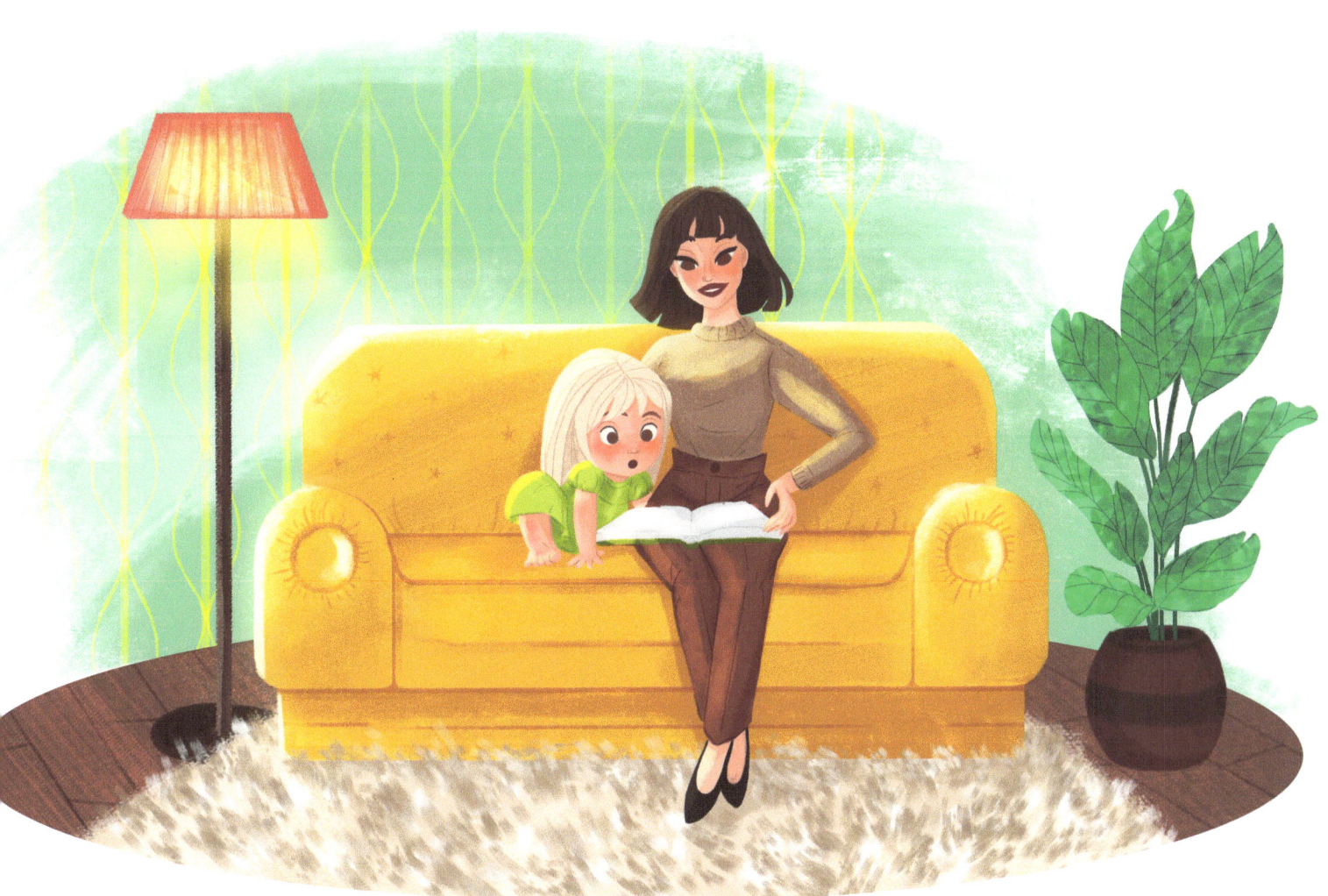

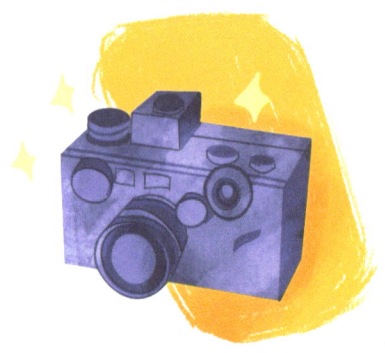

Her Dad also loved to take pictures and make home movies.
And he collected many kinds of cameras!

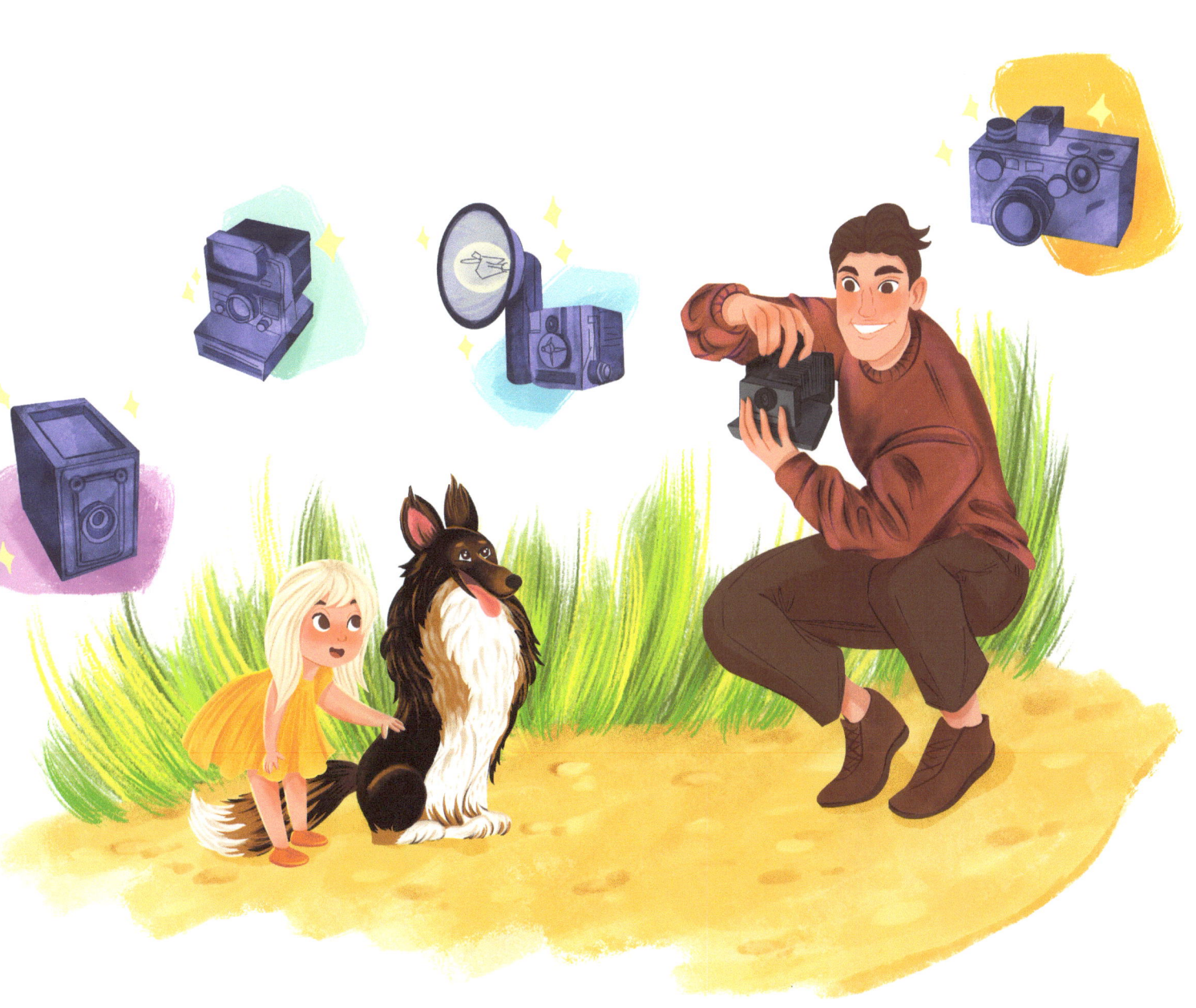

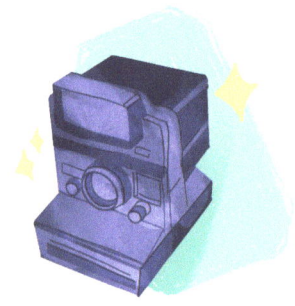

As she grew, Jean Ann started taking her own pictures. She took pictures of her family, friends and her pets and she began to make her own photo albums!

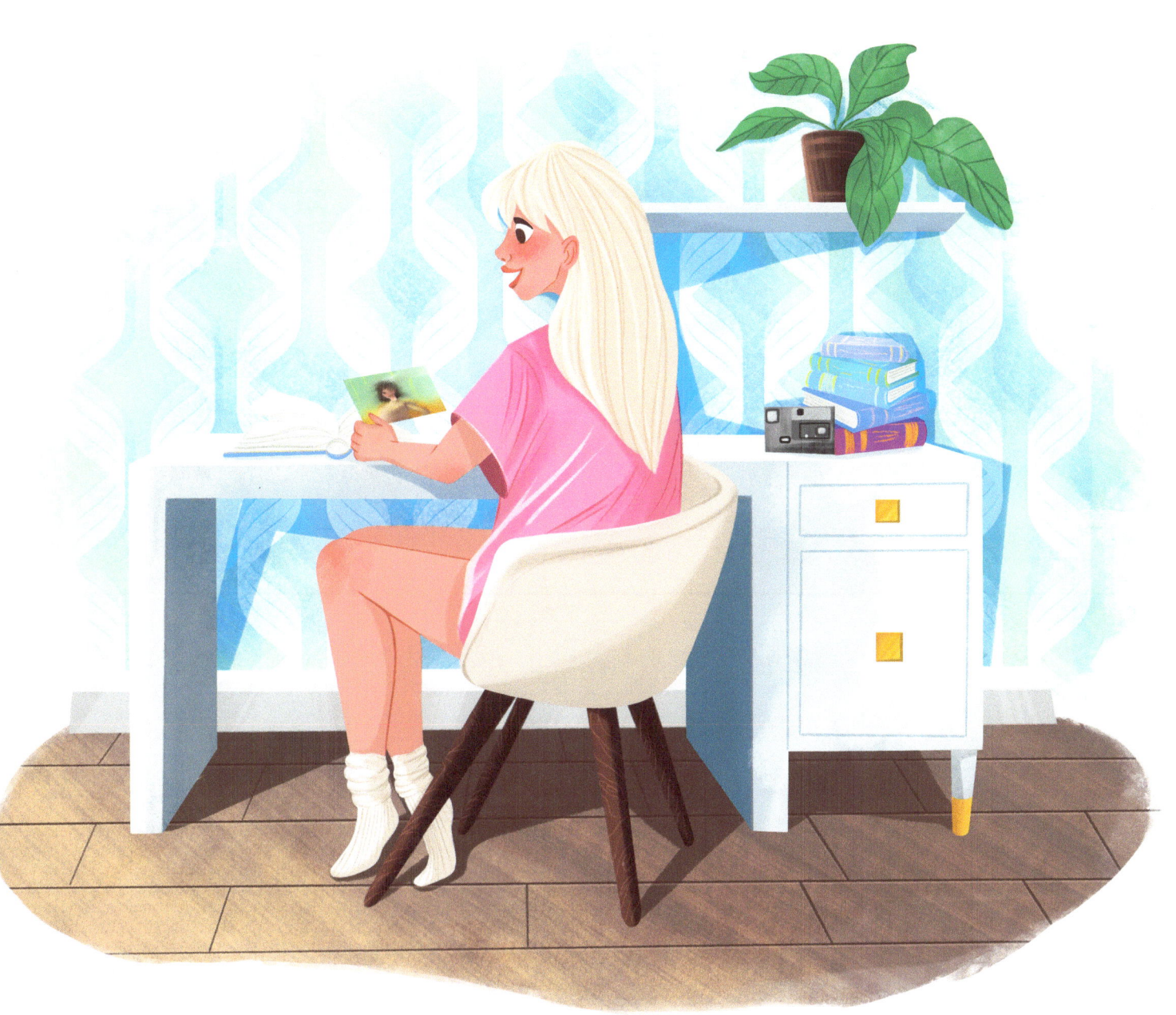

When she was all grown up, just like her Mom, she always took pictures of the people & things she loved!

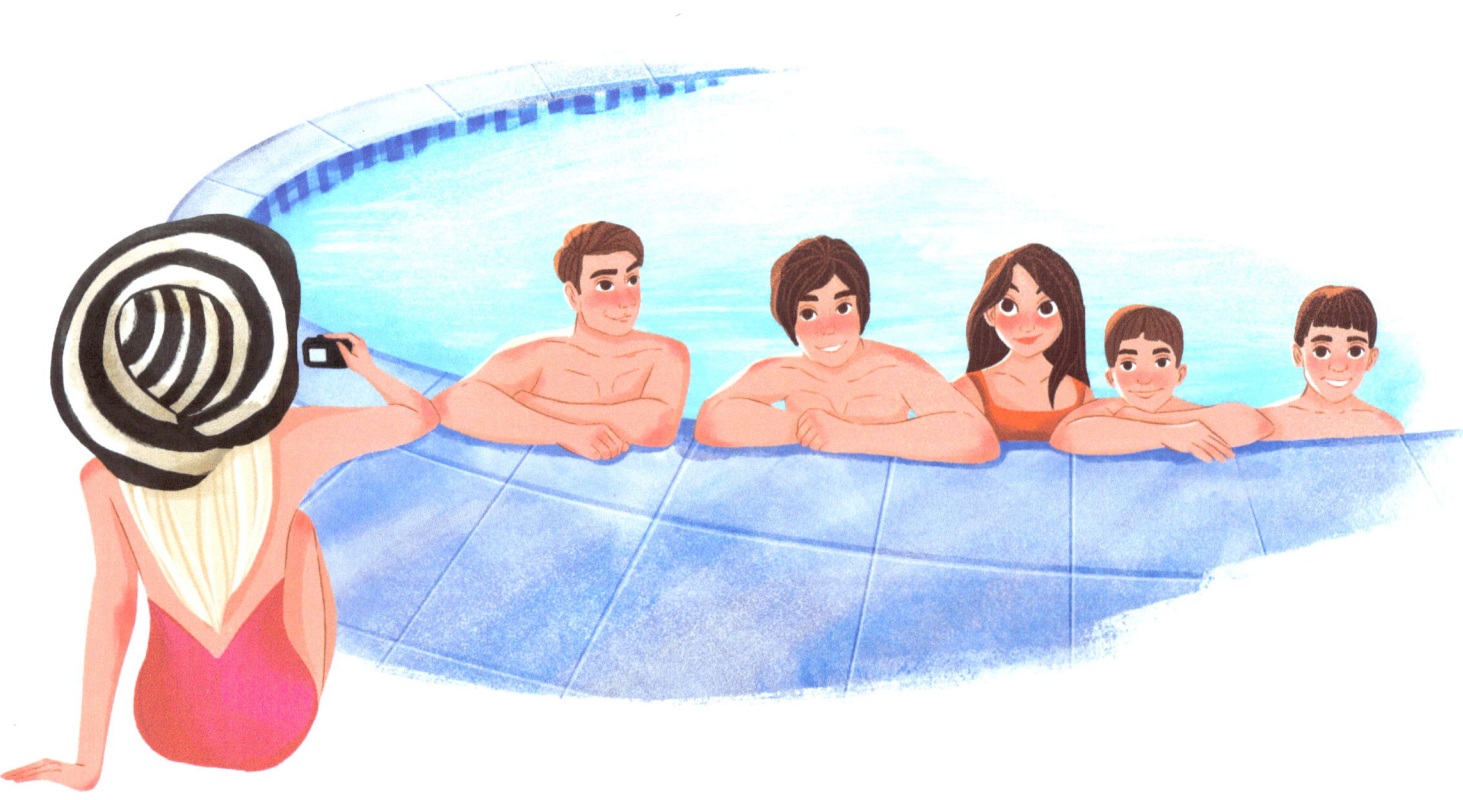

She took SO MANY pictures...Her husband bought her special bookshelves and sets of drawers to keep her many albums and pictures in!

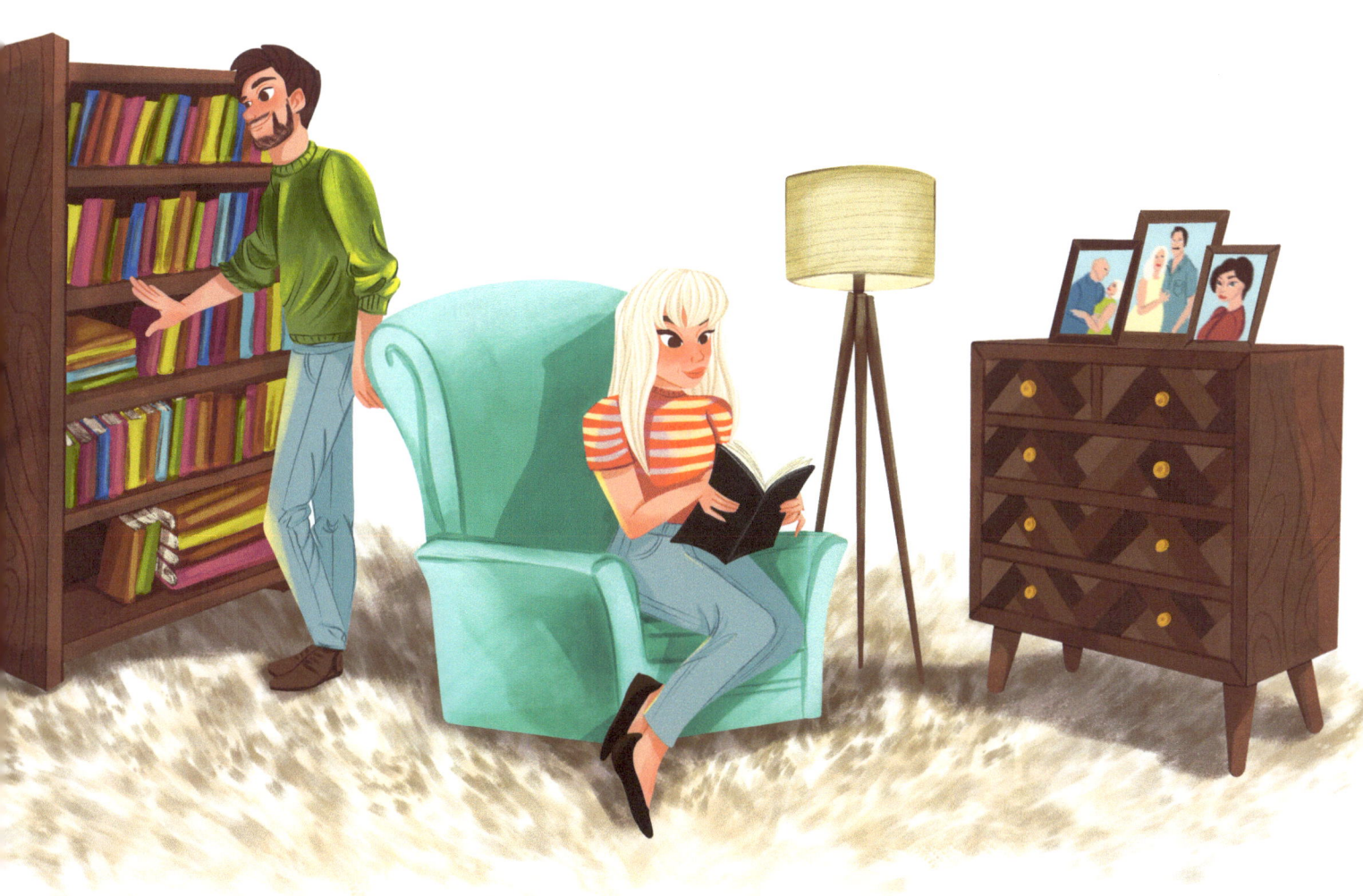

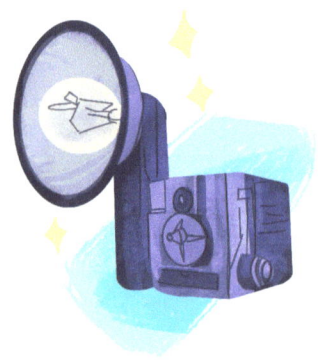

Jean Ann loved pictures so much!!
They brought her so much joy & happiness!!
She took pictures everywhere she went!!

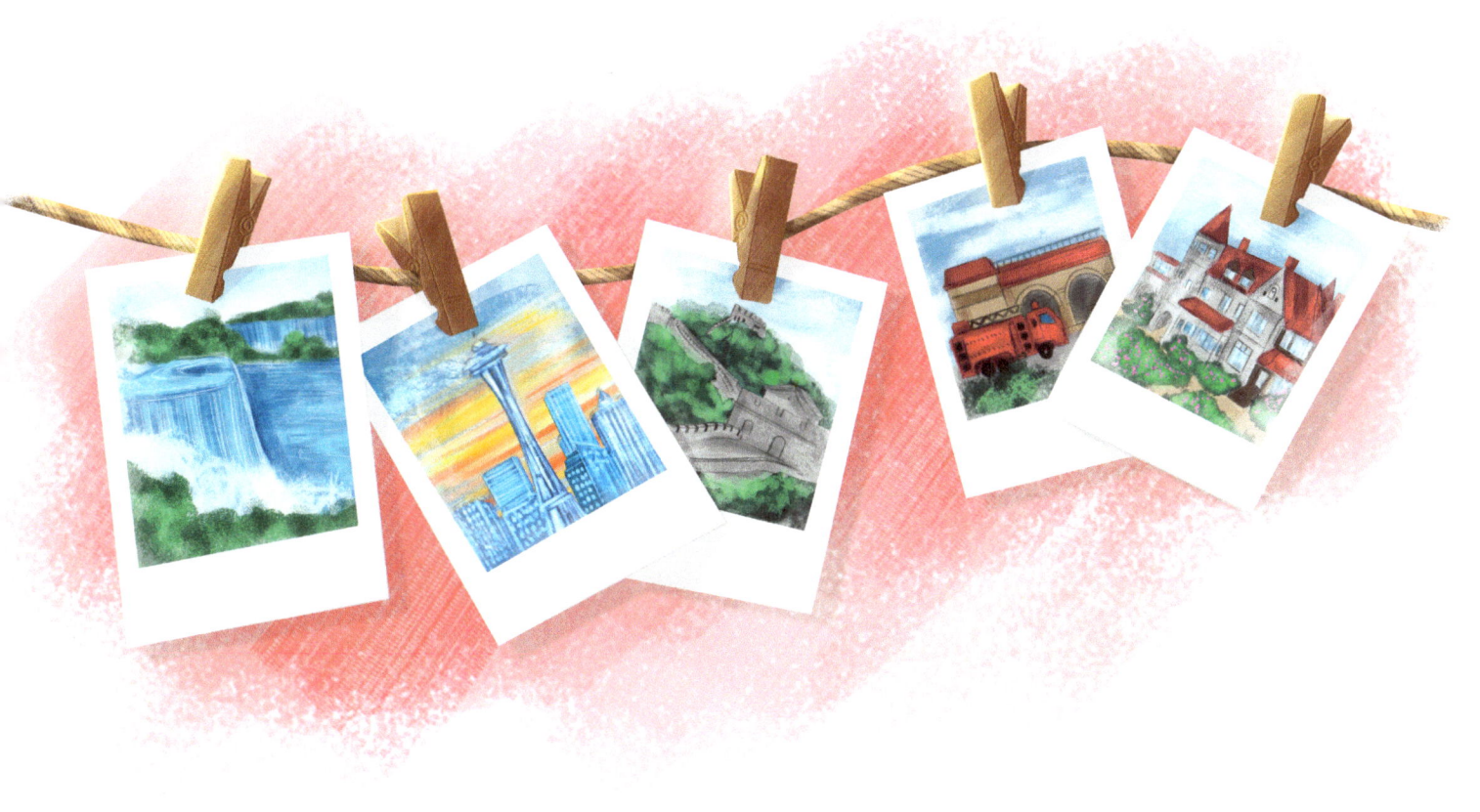

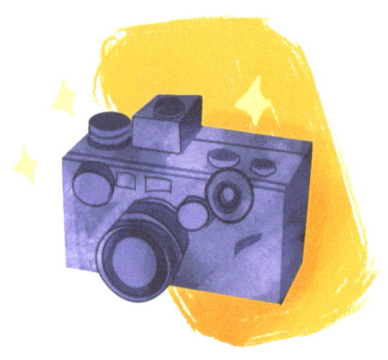

One of her children even grew up to be a professional photographer!! How Wonderful!!

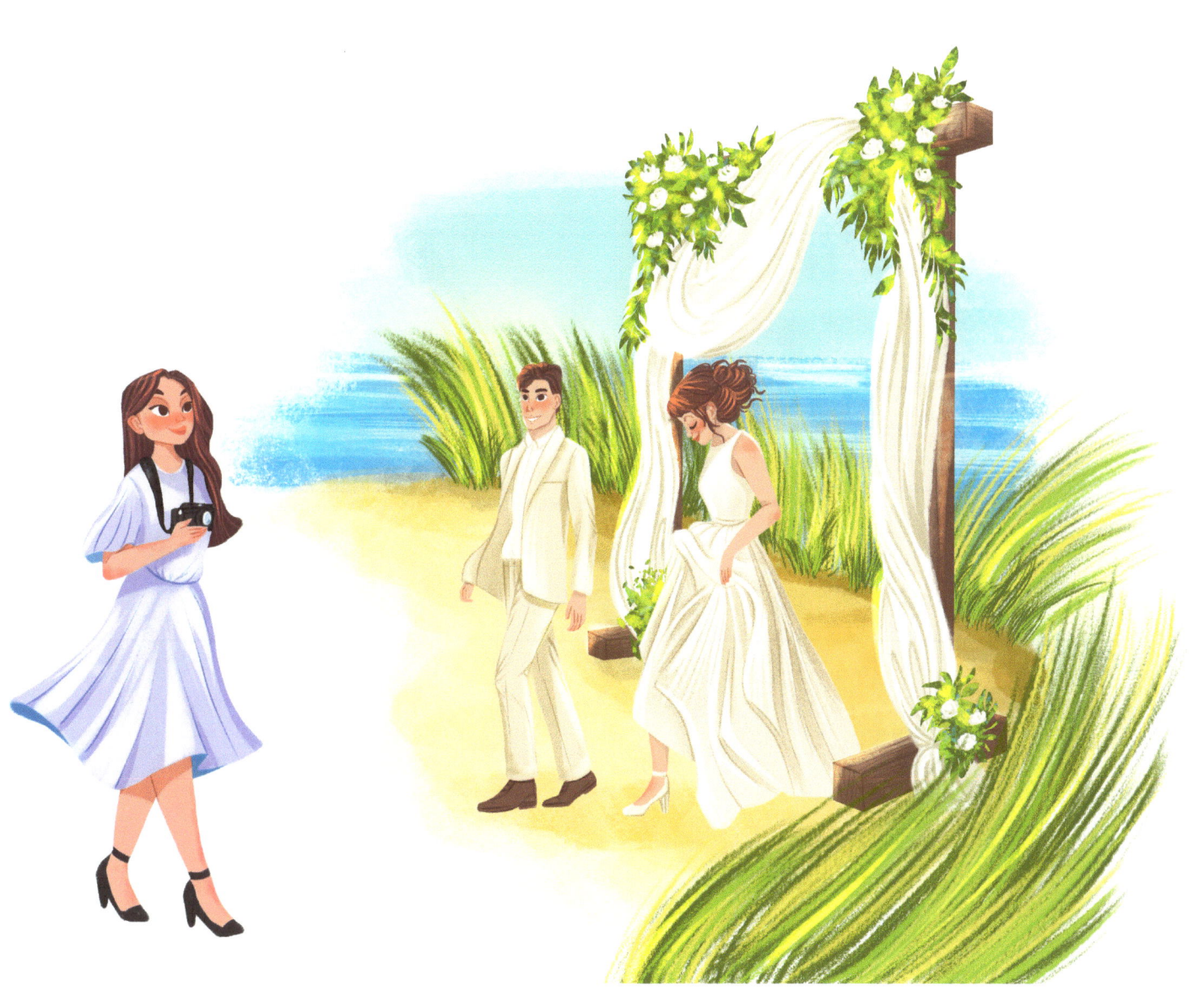

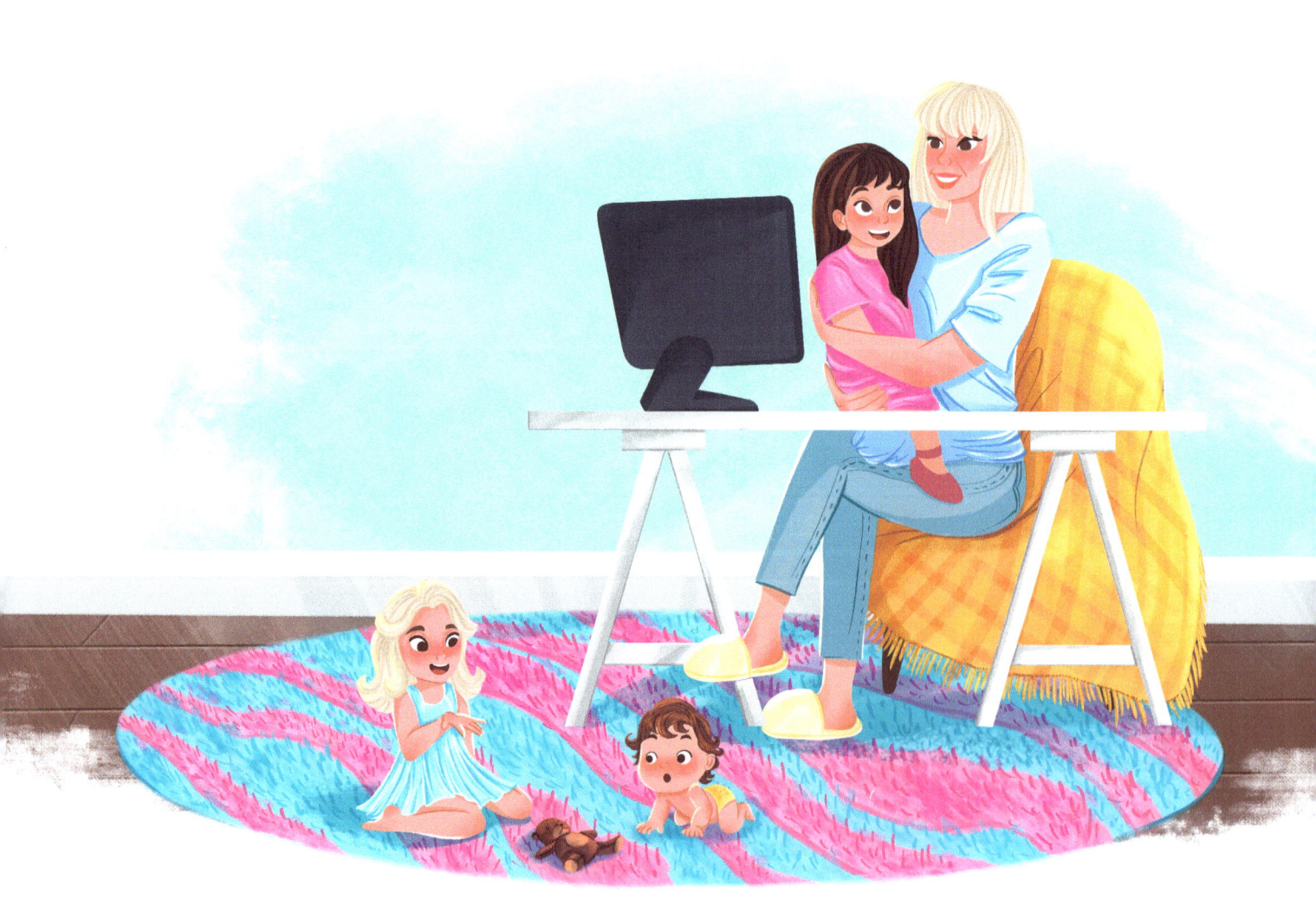

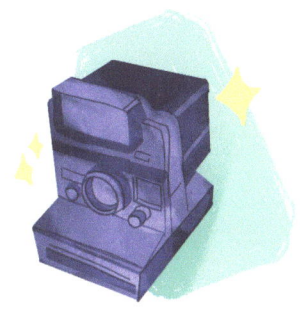

One day, Jean Ann's Granddaughter asked,
"Grandma, why do you love pictures so much?"
She replied, "Pictures capture moments & memories in time.
They remind me of people I love and treasured times spent with them.
And when we are far apart, pictures give us glimpses into each other's lives and keep us close in heart!"

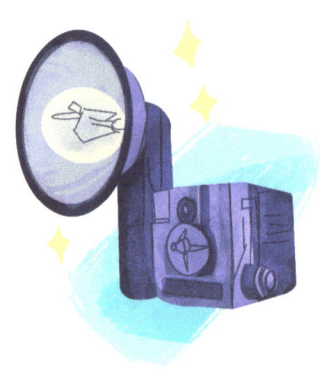

"I have a good idea Grandma! Let's take a picture together!"

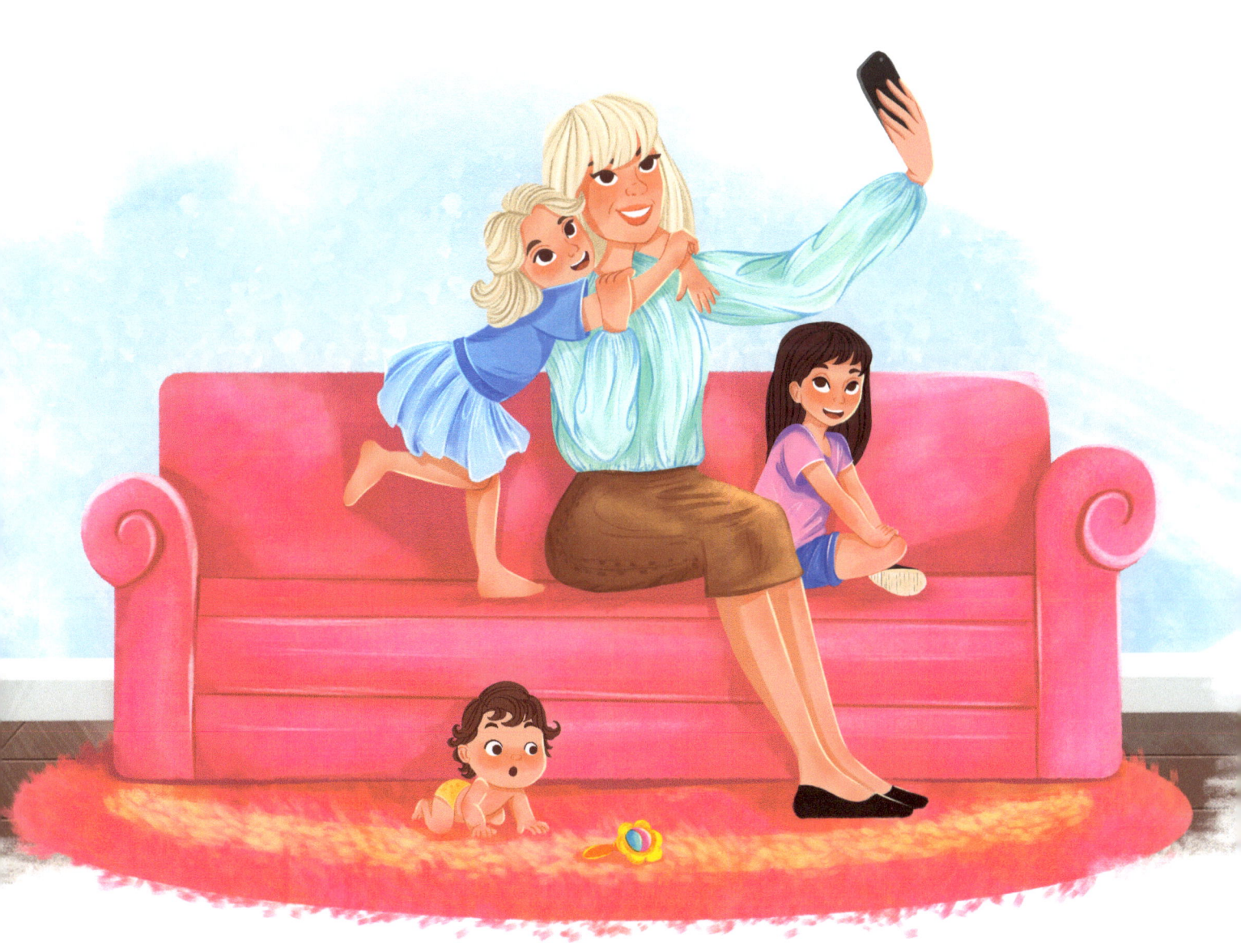

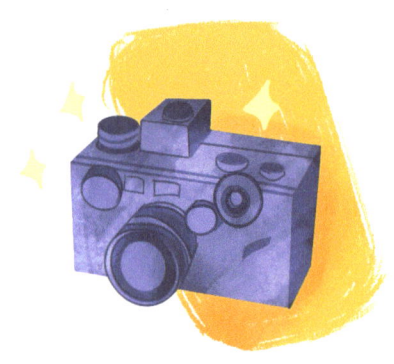

And Jean Ann replied,
"I think that is a GREAT idea!"

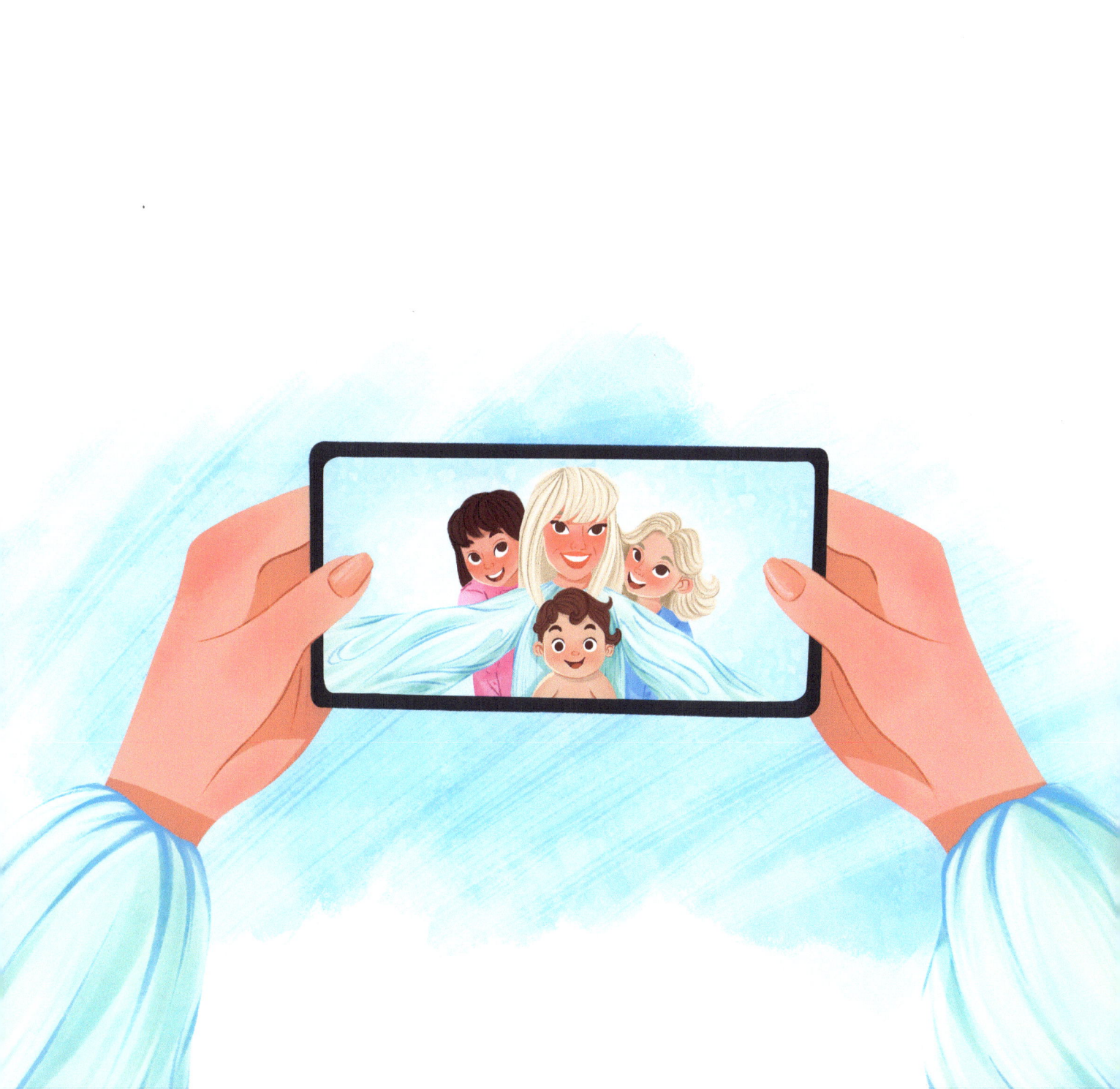

About the Author

Jeannie Schlatter is a Wife, Mom & Grandma. She loves her family with all of her being and praises God for each of them. She began taking pictures from a young age and often jokes that they will be her memory one day. She loves to care for others, drink coffee and travel....and of course take pictures of everything along the way!

"We will tell the next generation the praiseworthy deeds of the Lord." Psalm 78:4b

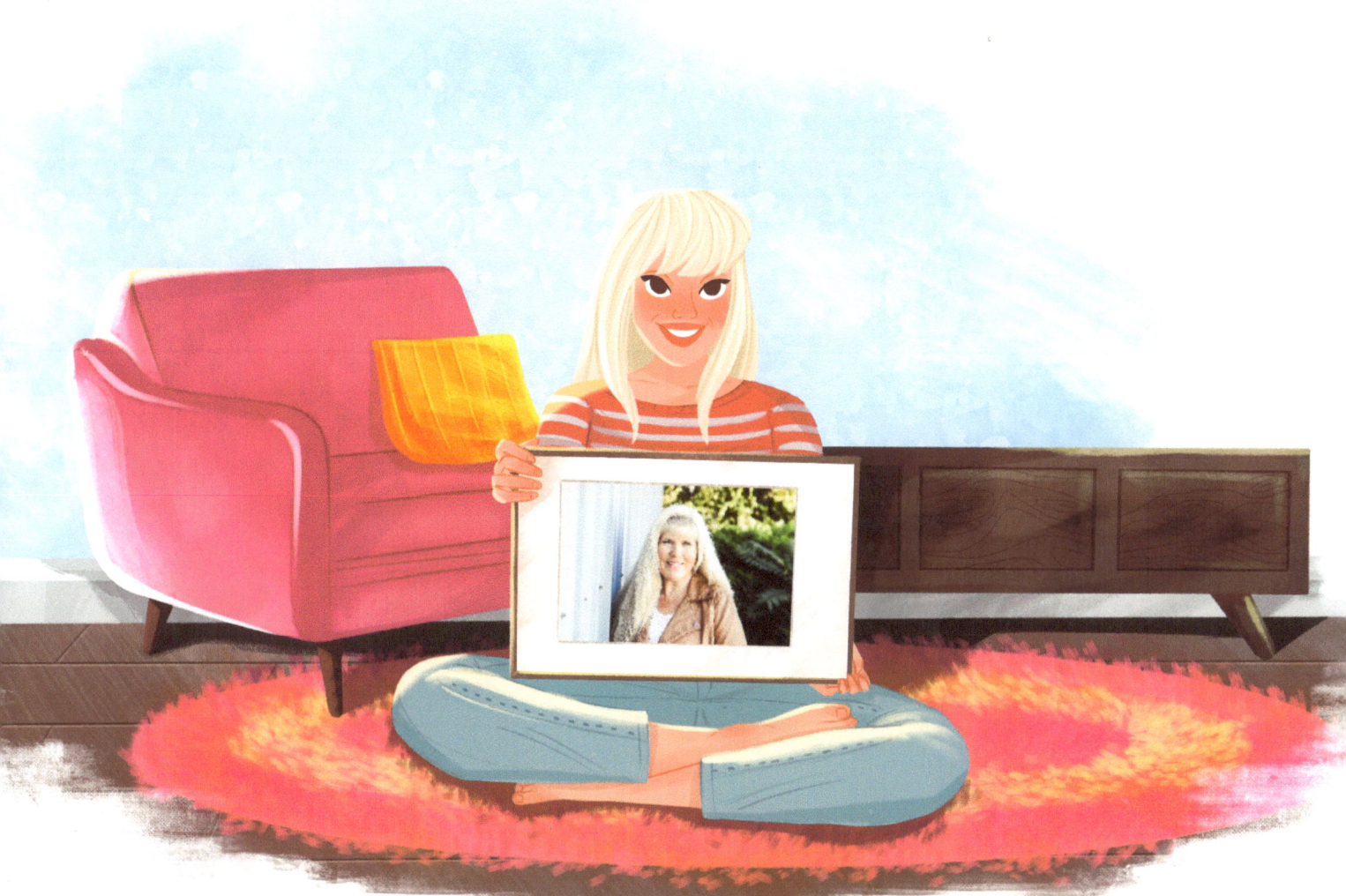

www.ingramcontent.com/pod-product-compliance
Lightning Source LLC
Chambersburg PA
CBHW051834210526
45473CB00005B/1873